A Crabtree Branches Book

TOP HORSE BREEDS
ARABIAN

Kerri Mazzarella

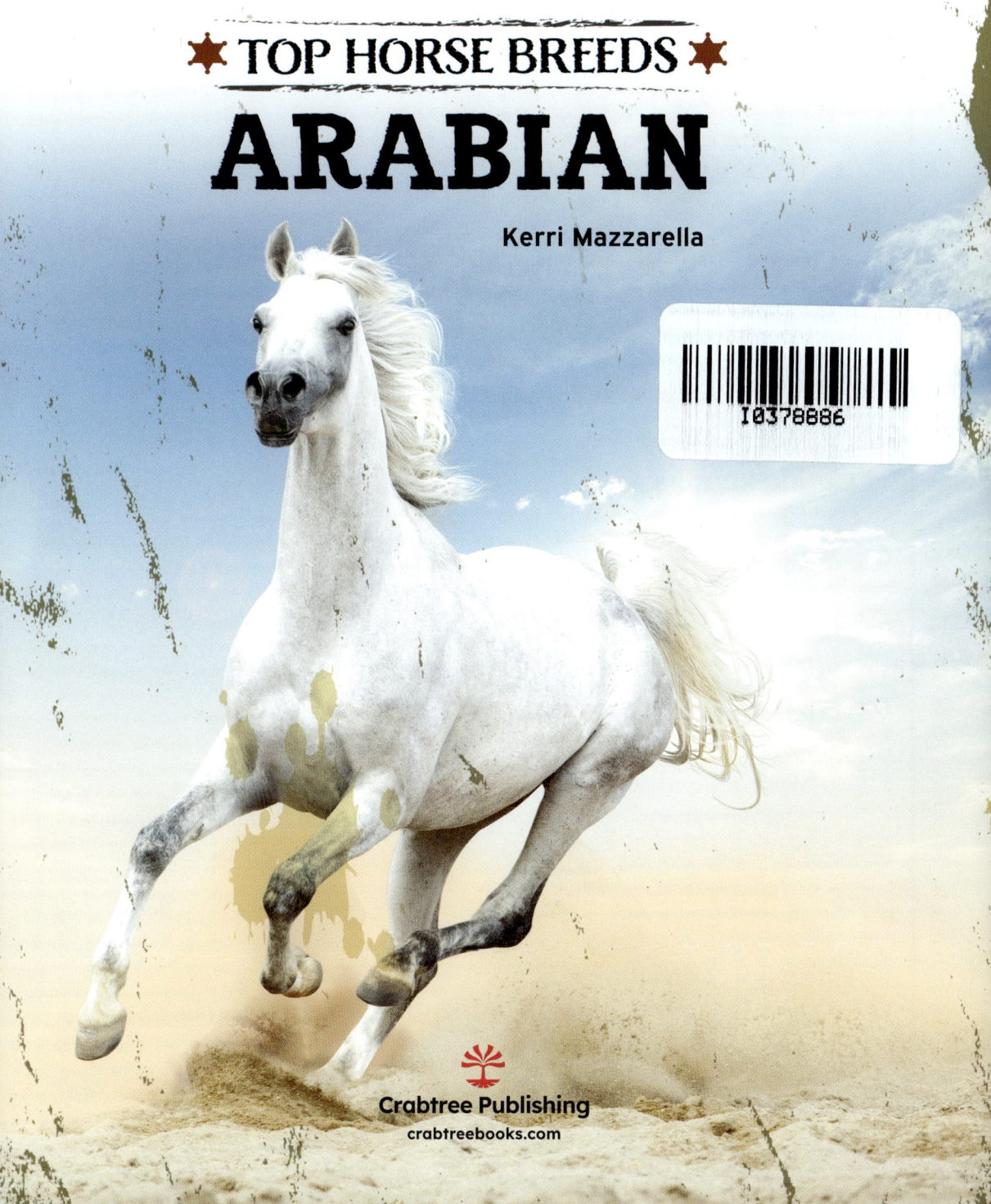

Crabtree Publishing
crabtreebooks.com

School-to-Home Support for Caregivers and Teachers

This high-interest book is designed to motivate striving students with engaging topics while building fluency, vocabulary, and an interest in reading. Here are a few questions and activities to help the reader build upon his or her comprehension skills.

Before Reading:
- What do I think this book is about?
- What do I know about this topic?
- What do I want to learn about this topic?
- Why am I reading this book?

During Reading:
- I wonder why...
- I'm curious to know...
- How is this like something I already know?
- What have I learned so far?

After Reading:
- What was the author trying to teach me?
- What are some details?
- How did the photographs and captions help me understand more?
- Read the book again and look for the vocabulary words.
- What questions do I still have?

Extension Activities:
- What was your favorite part of the book? Write a paragraph on it.
- Draw a picture of your favorite thing you learned from the book.

TABLE OF CONTENTS

History 4

Characteristics 8

Size and Color 12

Care and Feeding 16

Uses, Jobs, and Equipment 20

Cost 24

The G.O.A.T.s 28

Glossary 30

Index 31

Websites to Visit 31

About the Author 32

HISTORY

Arabian horses are one of the oldest **purebred** horse **breeds** in the world. They are beautiful and graceful horses. They **originated** in the Arabian Peninsula thousands of years ago.

Arabian horses were bred to survive the harsh desert climate. They were prized by the Bedouin, an Arab people who lived in the desert in tents. They often kept their Arabian horses in their family tents to keep them from getting harmed or stolen.

Napoleon Bonaparte

War and trade helped spread Arabian horses across Europe and around the globe. They were first brought to the United States in the 1700s.

Many historical figures, such as George Washington, Alexander the Great, and Napoleon Bonaparte, took pleasure in owning Arabian horses.

George Washington

DID YOU KNOW? The Arabian horse is known for its **stamina**, intelligence, and **agility**.

CHARACTERISTICS

The Arabian horse has a long, arched neck, a wedge-shaped head, and short, alert ears. Their eyes are large and set far apart. Arabians have large nostrils which help them take in lots of air! This can be helpful in hot desert environments.

Certain characteristics set Arabians apart from other horses. They have one less **vertebra** in their spine and one less pair of ribs than other breeds. Their tails sit higher than other horses too!

Arabian horses are known for their stamina when riding over long distances. They are highly intelligent and can be trained easily. They are generally social with people and other animals.

Arabians work better with skilled riders and trainers than with beginners. They are sensitive and can be stubborn at times. Their personalities are generally calm and pleasant.

DID YOU KNOW? Some Arabian horses will cause mischief or get into trouble when they are bored.

SIZE AND COLOR

The Arabian horse has a small, compact body and is generally smaller than many other breeds. They can range from 14 to 16 hands tall.

Arabians have a slender build but are very strong. They can weigh from 800 to 1,000 pounds (363 to 454 kg).

DID YOU KNOW? A horse's height is measured in hands. One hand is equal to 4 inches (10.2 cm).

The color of Arabian horses can vary. The most common colors are bay, gray, chestnut, and roan. Less common colors are black and white. Some Arabians have white markings on their faces and legs.

Sabino is a pattern found on some Arabians. It is a white-spotted pattern, usually on the face, belly, or upper legs.

DID YOU KNOW? All Arabian horses have black skin. The dark color helps protect Arabians from the harsh desert sun.

CARE AND FEEDING

Like all horses, Arabians eat a diet of grass, hay, barley, oats, and other grains. They love to eat fruits and vegetables for treats.

It is important that Arabians have plenty of fresh water available to drink. Horses can drink 10 to 12 gallons (38 to 45 L) a day!

Horses require shelter, **grooming**, and veterinary checkups. A barn or **stable** provides protection for horses during bad weather.

Grooming a horse is important for its overall health. Brushing and bathing a horse regularly keeps its skin and hair shiny and clean. Regular **hoof** care is important too! Did you know horses wear **horseshoes**?

DID YOU KNOW? Arabians are social horses. They love spending time with other horses in large, open pastures where they can run and graze on grass.

USES, JOBS, AND EQUIPMENT

Arabian horses can be found all over the world. The United States has more Arabians than any other country. Arabian horses are used for many different kinds of jobs.

Some Arabians are used by ranchers to work with cattle. They are also great for long-distance trail riding. Arabians are used for racing and **dressage** too.

It is important to have proper **horse tack** and safety equipment when dealing with any horse. They are strong, powerful animals that can cause serious injuries if not handled carefully.

Before handling a horse, taking horseback riding lessons from an experienced trainer is recommended. Always be sure to wear a helmet while riding.

COST

The cost of purebred Arabians can vary depending on factors such as age, gender, **bloodline**, color, and training. The average Arabian horse can range in price from $5,000 to $30,000.

Egyptian Arabian

Shagya Arabian

There are six types of purebred Arabian horses: Spanish, Russian, Egyptian, Polish, Shagya, and Crabbet. Although similar, each type has its own history and characteristics.

Owning a horse can be expensive. The average yearly cost to take care of a horse can range from $4,000 to $10,000. Housing is the greatest expense and can cost up to $6,000 a year.

Feeding a horse costs around $1,000 to $2,000 a year. Yearly costs for veterinary care can be around $750. Other expenses include grooming products, horse hoof maintenance, and riding equipment.

THE G.O.A.T.s

There have been many famous Arabian horses, but the greatest of all time is Marwan Al Shaqab. He has won many world championships. Someone once offered $20 million to buy him, but his owners refused!

Cass Ole is another famous Arabian horse. He had a fantastic show career and won many awards. He is best known for his role in the movie *The Black Stallion*.

GLOSSARY

agility (uh-JIL-i-tee): The ability to move quickly and easily

bloodline (BLUD-line): The ancestors of an animal

breed (BREED): A particular type of animal

dressage (druh-SAZH): A competition in which horses perform special movements based on signals from their riders

grooming (GROOM-ing): The practice of brushing and cleaning the coat of a horse, dog, or other animal

hoof (HOOF): The hard part that covers the feet of certain animals, such as horses

horse tack (HORS tak): The equipment used to handle and ride a horse

horseshoe (HORS-shoo): A U-shaped piece of metal nailed to the bottom of a horse's hoof to protect it

originated (or-IH-jin-ayt-ed): Began to exist or appear

purebred (PYOOR-bred): Having parents of the same breed

stable (STAY-buhl): A building where horses are fed and housed

stamina (STAM-uh-nuh): The energy and strength to keep doing something for a long time

vertebra (VUR-tuh-bruh): One of the small bones that form the spine

INDEX

Arabian Peninsula 4

color 14, 15, 24

cost 24, 26–27

desert 5, 8, 15

ears 8

grooming 18, 27

hay 16

height 12, 13

shelter 18

tail 9

water 17

weight 13

WEBSITES TO VISIT

www.thesprucepets.com/meet-the-arabian-horse-1886131

https://www.horseillustrated.com/enduring-arabian-horse

https://www.britannica.com/animal/Arabian-horse

ABOUT THE AUTHOR

Kerri Mazzarella lives in South Florida with her husband, four children, and two dogs. She loves horses and has always wanted to own one. Her daughter has taken horseback riding lessons for many years. She hopes you enjoy learning about different breeds of horses as much as she does!

Written by: Kerri Mazzarella
Designed by: Kathy Walsh
Series Development: James Earley
Proofreader: Melissa Boyce
Educational Consultant: Marie Lemke M.Ed.

Photographs: Shutterstock Cover & Title pg: Olga_i, benchart; Background and Border: benchart; p 4: pixinoo, Olga_i; p 6: @Wiki; p 7: Matt Snodderly; p 8: Makarova Viktoria; p 9 : Azahara Perez; p 10: Andrzej Kubik; p 12-13 Tamara Didenko; p 14-15: anakondasp; p 16: Sharon Morris; p 17: Alexia Khruscheva; p 18 Carlo Prearo; p 19 Olga_i; p 20 Sukhanova Daria; p 21: Dennis W Donohue; p 22: CatwalkPhotos; p 23: horsemen; p 24: Laila Kazakevica; p 25: horsemen; p 26: acceptphoto; p 29: Olga_i

Crabtree Publishing

crabtreebooks.com 800-387-7650
Copyright © 2024 Crabtree Publishing
All rights reserved. No part of this publication may be reproduced, stored in a retrieval system or be transmitted in any form or by any means, electronic, mechanical, photocopying, recording, or otherwise, without the prior written permission of Crabtree Publishing.

Printed in the U.S.A./072023/CG20230214

Published in Canada
Crabtree Publishing
616 Welland Ave.
St. Catharines, Ontario
L2M 5V6

Published in the United States
Crabtree Publishing
347 Fifth Ave
Suite 1402-145
New York, NY 10016

Library and Archives Canada Cataloguing in Publication
Available at Library and Archives Canada

Library of Congress Cataloging-in-Publication Data
Available at the Library of Congress

Hardcover: 978-1-0398-0940-6
Paperback: 978-1-0398-0993-2
Ebook (pdf): 978-1-0398-1099-0
Epub: 978-1-0398-1046-4